Healing

INSIGHTS

BIBLE STUDIES FOR GROWING
FAITH

———

Donna Schaper

THE PILGRIM PRESS
Cleveland

To those who are *well* even though *sick*.

The Pilgrim Press, 700 Prospect Avenue, Cleveland, Ohio 44115-1100
thepilgrimpress.com
© 2006 by The Pilgrim Press
All rights reserved. Published 2006

Scripture quotations are from the *New Revised Standard Version Bible*
copyright © 1989 by the Division of Christian Education of the National
Council of the Churches of Christ in the USA. Used by permission.

Printed in the United States of America on acid-free paper

10   09   08   07   06   5   4   3   2   1

Library of congress Cataloging-in-Publication Data

Schaper, Donna.
  Healing / Donna Schaper.
      p. cm. -- (Insights)
  Includes bibliographical references and index.
  ISBN-13: 978-0-8298-1703-4 (alk. paper)
  1. Healing--Religious aspects--Christianity. 2. Healing--Biblical
teaching. 3. Spiritual healing. I. Title.
  BT732.E66 2006
  234'.131--dc22
                        2006025632

Contents

Your Faith
Has Made You Well

Everybody will be *sick sometime*. Or suffer a debilitating accident. Or know someone who has been ill or hurt.

Everybody can also be *well all the time* — if we define "wellness" as faith, trust and peace.

Whether or not our bodies are ailing, whether or not physical improvement is taking place, this wellness takes place behind and before cure.

These five studies on healing take seriously Jesus' statement, "Your faith has made you well." They are for people who are interested in wellness. They are for people who find themselves surrounded by disease. They are also for people who are currently "well" but who want to develop a spiritual pattern of living that will assist them when they do confront trouble.

The purpose is to shift us from preoccupation with *cure* to preoccupation with *faith*. It is a proactive strategy for life-long wellness, even in the face of illness.

When we have faith, we are well.

Some Practical Matters

The issues of sickness and health, disease and cure, are up close and personal. We have all been affected by illness at times — and, some people, way more than others. And we each have a wide range of emotional, physical, and spiritual responses.

When we are well, we tend to put some distance between us and people who are sick. Maybe it's fear: It could happen to us. Maybe it's discomfort: We don't know what to say.

A similar distancing happens when we are sick, or close to some who is ill. The "outside" world comes to a stop and all that matters is what's happening in the hospital room, doctor's office, or sick room. During those times, we may wonder how anyone could possibly understand what we're going through. We may envy other people's freedom to make plans or go places, or we may cringe when someone says the "wrong" thing.

Whatever your experience has been, or is currently, with illness, I encourage you to listen with both your head and your heart to where other people are in their journeys.

The stories of Jesus are a place for us to meet, to look at what "wellness" really means. This book is an invitation to gather in a safe place, bring your questions, and come to some new understandings.

Here are some suggestions for proceeding with each session:

- Decide on "ground rules" for the group concerning confidentiality, so that people will feel free to speak openly.

- Set the tone for sharing. (Generally, people will not share more deeply than the group leader.)

- Reassure people that questions are good; answers are not necessary. This is a time for thoughts and ideas, not for deciding what's "right" and "wrong."

- Agree on a specific time frame for your sessions. This will help those with family commitments, baby-sitters, etc. make plans.

Here are some ideas for getting group members involved:

- Ask one person (ahead of time) to share their personal response to the chapter at the outset of the session.

- Ask people to watch for media stories during the week that relate to the chapter and bring them to share with the group.

- Ask someone to read aloud the scripture passage for the chapter at the beginning of each session. (You may want to explore other biblical translations as well; the quotations in this book are from the *New Revised Standard Edition*.)

- Have the group read the prayer for each chapter in unison at the end of the session.

Each session begins with a story from the Gospels, includes some thoughts about the passage, and ends with questions for individual reflection or group discussion. Ask people to read the material before your group meets and to use the Gospel story to consider what Jesus means by "healing."

What Is Wellness?

THE GOOD SAMARITAN

He asked Jesus, "Who is my neighbor?"

Jesus replied, "A man was going down from Jerusalem to Jericho, and fell into the hands of robbers, who stripped him, beat him, and went away, leaving him half dead. Now by chance a priest was going down that road; and when he saw him, he passed by on the other side. So likewise a Levite, when he came to the place and saw him, passed by on the other side. But a Samaritan while traveling came near him; and when he saw him, he was moved with pity. He went to him and bandaged his wounds, having poured oil and wine on them. Then he put him on his own animal, brought him to an inn, and took care of him. The next day he took out two denarii, gave them to the innkeeper, and said, 'Take care of him; and when I come back, I will repay you whatever more you spend.' Which of these three, do you think, was a neighbor to the man who fell into the hands of the robbers?"

He said, "The one who showed him mercy."

Jesus said to him, "Go and do likewise."

–Luke 10:30-37

Most of us have read or heard a health warning sometime in the last week — usually in the form of "advertise-ese." Here are a few lines I picked up just from the magazines at my bedside:

> "Gum Disease: The Silent Killer"
> "The Perils of Throw Rugs"
> "What You Don't Know about Pâté"
> "Hepatitis: The Insidious Spread of a Killer Virus"
> "If you don't take potassium supplements, you are only fooling yourself."

Morning television is a consistent alternation of news stories and health stories, most about weight, some about life-threatening diseases and how to prevent them. Wellness, in the guise of threatening sickness, is the key feature story of our age.

The problem is not our wish to be "well," but our definition of "wellness." To understand wellness, we must comprehend both the Kevins and Deris of the world. Kevin is a man in my congregation who has lived with an active brain tumor and thirteen surgeries, eighteen chemos, and eleven radiations for twelve years. A woman in my congregation, Deri, died after three years of fighting stomach cancer. Both experienced various forms of wellness — *if* we understand wellness as both a physical and a spiritual matter, simultaneously.

Jesus constantly mixed body and soul. He didn't diminish body or elevate soul so much as he saw the whole person. He understood that spiritual dis-ease is as difficult as physical dis-ease, that we suffer even though we are not blind, lame, or mentally ill. There is more than one way to be sick, which suggests that there is more than one way to be well. People can be cured of their leprosy but sick with ingratitude. People can be blind and still be well.

I once met a man on a train to Vancouver. He was blind. Yet he was pointing out to me all the things he could not see, except in his memory of many trips. His accuracy for waterfalls and large stone outcroppings was astonishing. I have never been able to read the scriptures about Jesus healing the blind man without thinking of this man on the train. His sight was not cured or returned, but he was very well. He had found another way to be well. The loss of his sight had not destroyed him. He was no longer perfect or complete, but he was well. I believe this message is what we need to chase fear from our door: *We can be well even if we are physically sick.*

For many of us, this requires a shift in our thinking.

Not everyone's cancer can be *cured*, and the good news is that we don't need to be cured to be *well*. When Jesus says, "Your faith has made you well," is it not possible he is saying that wellness is the capacity to trust? That wellness is not the absence of disease but the presence of faith? Such a faith has many advantages, in addition to the simplicity of its definition. We can be dying from cancer and still trust in God and trust in our future.

If we truly believe that wellness is not the same as cure (although it may include cure), that means *we can achieve wellness with or without cure.* When we are "well" in the larger sense of the word, we have the courage to move into the future, whether that future is death, diminished life or healed life. Whatever life we have biologically can be redeemed.

Jesus said that he came so we could have life, and have it abundantly (John 10:10). If that isn't a definition of wellness, I don't know what is.

Wellness is the act of trust and faith in our well-being, no matter what happens to our body or our loved ones.

This more complete view of wellness has ramifications not only for those who are sick, but for those who want to help them. In story after story of Jesus' healing, Jesus positioned himself as more than a physical healer. His compassion spilled into the needs of the people.

Think of the classic "Good Samaritan" story. We've heard it many times, and taken to heart its message that we are to reach out and help others in need. But have we really heard its message that the spiritual side (the Good Samaritan's compassion) is as important as the physical side (his binding of the wounds and payment to innkeeper)? Do we *really* understand that "caring" is different from "curing"?

In truth, we are never actually told whether the beaten man heals or not. The point of the story is not the outcome but the process.

Process matters. How we get there matters. The roads we take, the gifts we give matter.

You've heard the saying, "It's not what you say, but the way you say it." Tone of voice really does matter. Even when we can control little else, we can manage our personal tone. We find ourselves well when we can be nice to the nurses, decent to the doctors, welcoming to visitors — even if our diagnosis is terrible and we can't sleep. We can still give gifts no matter how much we hurt.

I think of Mary at eighty-nine. She had an arthritis that hurt her all the time. She still drove, but was so osteoporotic that she peered through the steering wheel rather than over it. I was staying at a hotel in her town and wanted to visit her. I said I would take a cab to her so that she would not have to drive. She absolutely refused, insisting, as I knew she would, that she would be the hospitable one. As I watched her drive up to the hotel parking lot and saw her hunched over the wheel, it dawned on me that she was doing exactly what she wanted to do. She wanted to come see me, and she didn't want to "bother" me. She wanted to give the gift. I'll bet she was scared driving there. I'll also bet her arthritis hurt her that day. But I never heard a word about her troubles. Instead, I heard about her joy that we had a chance for a visit.

Even if we cannot manage the outcome, we can manage the process. And the process, in turn, assists the outcome because process takes the burden off destiny and places the burden on journey. It is rarely where we end up that matters! What matters is how we get there, what turns in the road we choose to take and which we do not.

The journey toward wellness is always possible.

Questions for Reflection and Discussion

1. What does "wellness" mean to you?

2. What is your response to the statement, "Wellness is not the absence of disease but the presence of faith"?

3. How do you think spiritual wellness and physical wellness are linked?

4. When have you experienced both physical and spiritual caring from someone? How did both contribute to your well-being?

5. Have you seen a person who is sick demonstrate wellness? What "gifts" have you received from someone who was hurting?

Where could your "tone" make a difference? What gift could you give, even if you are tired or in poor health?

* * *

A PRAYER FOR WELLNESS

There will be days when we won't be able to be well. Reassure us that the darkness is a place for germination. Let us be comfortable in the dark and refuse to put up the sign on our door that we are "Closed after Dark." Help us learn to love night thoughts, the way we love stars. Show us how the seeds germinate, and return us from doubt to faith, despair to hope, sickness to wellness. Amen.

What Is Healing?

Jesus' Teaching in the Synagogue

When he came to Nazareth, where he had been brought up, he went to the synagogue on the sabbath day, as was his custom. He stood up to read, and the scroll of the prophet Isaiah was given to him. He unrolled the scroll and found the place where it was written: "The Spirit of the Lord is upon me, because he has anointed me to bring good news to the poor. He has sent me to proclaim release to the captives and recovery of sight to the blind, to let the oppressed go free, to proclaim the year of the Lord's favor."

And he rolled up the scroll, gave it back to the attendant, and sat down. The eyes of all in the synagogue were fixed on him. Then he began to say to them, "Today this scripture has been fulfilled in your hearing."

–Luke 4:16-21

Whenever I preached a healing story in my congregation in Miami, Nathan's mom, Peggy, was probably there. Nathan has a fast growing brain tumor; he lost his balance two weeks before his eighteenth birthday and has been on chemo ever since. Charlotte, John's widow, might also have been in attendance. John died of lung cancer after a long life in the theater. Another dozen or so women who had breast cancer and survived might have been present, as would have been four women currently in treatment.

They call themselves "the hairless wonders." The congregants would also know that the woman preaching has faced breast cancer herself. Some men might have thought about their prostates when I spoke of Jesus' healing. Those who didn't have cancer might have been afraid of those who did. Or wondered why this very common disease had not yet struck them — and when it would.

When we hear a story about healing, we are not hearing it in a vacuum. We are hearing about something we might either directly experience or indirectly fear. As we age, our fascination with health will only increase. There is a wide consensus that people would rather die than live distorted or disabled lives. We want "health span" as much as "lifespan." "As long as I have my health" is as long as most people want to live.

If "wellness" is the feature story in many magazines, "health care" is the feature story of all too many business reports. While religious traditions are unanimously in favor of wellness, spiritually and physically, we still live in a society where healing is bought and sold. Today we speak of the "health care industry" without blinking an eye. We have even forgotten to be offended that *caring* is an *industry.*

In the background of every healing story is the fear about money and health: How much do we need to get medical attention? What if we lose our job? Or what if we can't leave the lousy job we have because we need it for the insurance? Health and healing is mixed up with costs, and money is joining illness in being an anxiety-maker for most.

There are also generational issues with regard to health issues, as this *New York Times* review of Gina Kolata's book *The Quest for Truth about Exercise and Health* points out:

> A generation that set out to change the world...soon focused instead on changing themselves — inside and out. Over the last twenty

years...the educated upper middle class spent
more and more time seeking personal salvation
on treadmills, elliptical, life cycles, Stairmasters
and other sophisticated machines.

Boomers use health as a way to control a life that admits
of very little other control. Seniors face genuine health
issues. X and Y generations know there won't be money for
their health care, social security, or maintenance. When
we add up all the messages about health concerns, it is no
surprise that we have become obsessed with healing and
staying well.

One has only to attend the average Protestant worship
service in which the prayers of the people are elicited to
hear the linguistic creep of the word "healing." It is used
for everything from cancer to sadness to divorce to college
rejections. The word "healing" is everywhere. But there is
a lot of confusion between "healing" and "curing."

If we accept the idea that there is more than one way to
be well, then there certainly are many forms of healing.
Don't you suppose that Jesus had this in mind when he
spoke at the synagogue about his own mission: *"to bring
good news to the poor, to proclaim release to the captives
and recovery of sight to the blind, to let the oppressed go
free"*? One of the ways Jesus demonstrated healing, as
opposed to curing, was by seeing humans as whole per-
sons. He did not distinguish physical healing from emotional and spiritual healing. He offered rest to all who were
weary, living water to any who would drink of it, food for
all who were hungry, shelter to all who were lost.

Healing begs for a redefinition.

One form of healing, for example, is to be aware of the
rest of the world while you struggle with a catheter. Or to
be able to laugh at your bathroom shelf overflowing with
hair products while your hair is falling out. Or to be able
to listen to someone's distress over a problem kid while

your own kids are wondering how much longer you'll be around.

Or to remain capable of caring for another. When a congregation prays every night at 9 p.m. (or some stated time) for those mentioned on Sunday morning, a spiritual laying on of hands and attention can happen.

Or to face death without fear. As the Psalmist said, "Your love, O God, is greater than life to me." Robbing death of its power to frighten us is a strong way to be well.

Unfortunately, sickness causes us to be even more self-obsessed than we already are. Luther's definition of sin, *"incurvatus in se,"* ("curved in on self") becomes even more profound.

Don was one of those who forgot to be curved in on himself. He had been very ill and was hospitalized for six weeks. Whenever I visited him, he was usually listening to opera tapes, and he always wanted to know if anyone was praying for him. He kept assuring me that the combination of operas' great emotion and prayers' great accompaniment were the reasons he was so well, even though he was still pretty sick.

When he finally got home, he remarked about the importance of being able to walk two blocks — and how he had always taken that walk and his capacity to do it for granted before. He whispered to me that the terrible six weeks may have been a gift to him: Now he knew not to take so much for granted. Now he knew the power of prayer.

Don forgot to be curved in on himself.

Esther was just the opposite. Every time anyone visited her in the hospital, she was so obnoxious that she drove people away. She complained. She guilt-tripped those who had only "breezed in and out." She demanded things. She said the coffee we brought from what used to be her favorite coffee shop was terrible. Her illness had turned her in on herself, and she was stuck in there. Usually I leave hospital visits inspired by the person whom I have visited. They "heal" me by their courage. Esther does not. She is a stranger to healing. Even if she does shake her heart problem, she probably won't ever be well.

We talk about the importance of the moment. But many of us get stuck so deeply inside ourselves that we miss our moments. Esther's fear and anxiety had taken all her good moments away from her. Don's calm and openness (and maybe the opera) had given him his good moments.

There is, as Walter Brueggeman puts it, a capacity in us, by the grace of God in Jesus, to live blessedly assured during a blessed disturbance. With the Psalmist, we can rejoice in relationship with God on this side, the other side, in the dark side and in the bright side. We can live with this assurance:

> When you pass through the waters, I will be with you; and through the rivers, they shall not overwhelm you. (Isaiah 43:1)

Healing is both a biological and a spiritual process. Healing takes time; it is developmental and progressive. Those who are prepared for healing know about slowness and are not afraid of it. We know about scabs and we know about bruises. We know about the slow changes to our bodies over time-both the detrimental and the wonderful. Those who know about healing do not confuse wellness with cure.

Ultimately, *healing is the journey toward wellness, with or without cure.*

Questions for Reflection and Discussion

1. What are your major concerns about wellness and healing?

2. How do you see the difference between "curing" and "healing"?

3. How do you feel after you've been with a person who has forgotten to be "curved in on themselves"? How is this a gift of healing?

4. When are you most likely to "curve in on yourself?" How can you imagine shifting that curve outward?

5. Where you see healing happening around you? Within you?

Where do you see the need for more healing? How might you contribute to the process?

* * *

A PRAYER FOR HEALING

Bring us light to see what is missing or hidden,
 to see what is neglected or forgotten,
 to see what is ignored, both inside us and beyond.
Teach us by your light
 to trustingly see
 all that is well within us and around us.

Where Are the Miracles?

THE MAN BLIND FROM BIRTH

As he walked along, he saw a man blind from birth. His disciples asked him, "Rabbi, who sinned, this man or his parents, that he was born blind?"

Jesus answered, "Neither this man nor his parents sinned; he was born blind so that God's works might be revealed in him. We must work the works of him who sent me while it is day; night is coming when no one can work. As long as I am in the world, I am the light of the world."

When he had said this, he spat on the ground and made mud with the saliva and spread the mud on the man's eyes, saying to him, "Go, wash in the pool of Siloam" (which means Sent).

Then he went and washed and came back able to see.

–John 9:1-7

Miracles happen. But they don't happen to everybody. And therein lies the problem. If we've prayed for a miracle cure but haven't received it, we begin to ask ourselves the equivalent of the disciples' question of Jesus when he saw a man blind from birth: "Who sinned, that he was born blind?" We step into the finger-wagging context of "What did they do wrong?" We look for someone or something to blame.

Of course, our language might not be quite the same. We might be more likely to blame ourselves: "What have I done to deserve this?" or "I should have prayed harder." Or we blame the system: "The doctor should have caught this earlier" or "The drug companies shouldn't be making so much profit off of drugs that don't work."

The miracle approach creates fear and guilt: "If Jesus can heal, and if I am not cured, have I done something wrong? Am I my own worst enemy?"

The new-age wellness movements have only exacerbated the self-blame. They promise a cure if we take the *right* vitamins in the *right* ways at the *right* times. They imagine levels of cure that are not possible. Ask Deri: She died after three years of fighting her stomach cancer with "greens." Don't think my congregation didn't notice. One of them actually said to me, "I guess Deri just didn't have enough faith." I found that cruel to Deri. Molly Ivens, who has had breast cancer, likes to quip, "Cancer doesn't give a rat's a_ _ if you have a good mental attitude." I join many in appreciating her truth. I have accompanied way too many people to "the other side" who had excellent mental attitudes, including Deri.

In his excellent study *A New Christianity for a New World*, Bishop Spong argues, and I agree, that people who hang on to miracles are people who can't bear the vulnerability of living, which is the most Christ-like of all behaviors. Their immature dependence on a "Daddy God" actually is the opposite of faith, and inhibits mature trust.

Here's a thought to consider: Jesus is the reason for our wellness. In the end, it is not our faith that makes us well; it is the gift that he gives that lets us trust. His very affirmation of us becomes our affirmation of him.

This is a picture of mature trust. Mature trust understands that we, everything — animals, plants, and flowers — die. It is an insult to the great and beautiful limits of life to avoid the fact of death. Jesus himself would agree. Indeed, Jesus' death on the cross implies less of a fear of death than a fear of spiritual diminishments.

Mature trust understands the great majesty of germ and grain and the inspired pattern in creation. What matters is relationship with God, here and now. Mature trust uses both prayer and chemo as a way to help people get *well* when they are sick.

When we understand the "healing" in the stories of Jesus, honor nature and its limits, respect the limits of medical science, perhaps faith can even be trusted again.

This leads us to another tension in miracles: the whole area of control. Miracles are a reach for control from deep within human vulnerability. We would like to think we are in control of things that we do not, cannot, and should not control-even the power of our faith. You've probably seen them, the TV shows where someone preaches that, if you have enough faith, you will be well.

Let me be very careful here when I speak of faith healing. Books such as Jane Yoder's *The Radiation Sonnets* are an example of faith healing that is part of the ancient reliquarial model. She wrote these beautiful sonnets as a ritual of healing, one for every day of her husband's radiation and chemotherapy, as a way to know wellness while she was living in great pain and fear.

Then there are books that take the same thought-for-the day approach, but hold out the promise of health and prosperity. And if that doesn't come your way, the inherent message is that you need to re-double your efforts; you need to believe more, pray more. Surely some people are helped by these approaches. But most are failed by it when the cure doesn't come. And when the cure doesn't come, many of us can't inch our way back to faith. We get stranded in the miracle while healing possibilities abound all around us.

The bottom line is that if we can't "control" our illness — by finding a source to blame — then we can't "control" our cure. That leaves us with trying to understand the miracles stories of scripture with integrity. And because we can't figure out how to understand the miracle stories with integrity, we don't emphasize their great healing powers. They do *heal* us; they just don't *cure* us.

The way NOT to understand healing is to focus on the miracles. The reality is, as often as Jesus healed, he also advocated care for the un-cured, for those who had to live with the limits of their condition. This has profound implications. Maybe "curing" was never the main show! Maybe connecting, trusting, helping, loving, believing has more to do with healing than miracles. That doesn't mean we have to rule out curing. But it is a side show, not the main show, in the healing story.

A member of my congregation, aged sixty-seven, was recently told that he has incurable leukemia. (The doctors always pick such great language!) His brother was not a potential stem cell donor, he is not well enough to be entered into the national bank, and the government — on nearly the same day — decided to curtail stem cell research, citing ethical reasons. Tom (name, of course, changed) left the hospital after grueling weeks of chemo.

But the amazing thing is, he reports feeling more joy than he can remember in being alive, being able to use the subway, being able to hug his partner. He knows the true joy of being alive. He is *well* on so many levels!

When Tom and his partner came to visit, they brought with them plans for a beautiful memorial service. Over salads and lasagna, we put the final touches on it. None of us were happy about the activity, but we were happy to be together. We were happy to be able to do what we were doing. And the lasagna was really good — four cheeses blended together in a way that reminded all of us of the true joy of eating.

Some might see this as denial that death is coming. I see it as "denial" on behalf of life. I see it as a place of freedom. If we sat around thinking about the obvious fact that we will all die and that all of our days are numbered, we might never get to the lasagna. As it is, we get there. We eat. We commune with each other. We put one foot in front of the other on the way to the subway. We live. We know we are alive. Sometimes we know more about being alive when we are seeing our end than when we are not. There are a range of gifts to this "denial" on behalf of life. One of them is wellness.

Tom shows us a new version of mature trust, a new version of releasing control. He is not sitting around figuring out who sinned. He is not sitting around wasting what little time he has left. He is not insulting life by fearing death. Instead, he is doing what he has to do with the people with whom he must do it. He is engaged in living. He is relating. He is caring for his partner in a beautiful way. He is pointing to life. And he is teaching us all something about how to face our end time. The word is calm. The word is trust. The word is even joy.

Questions for Reflection and Discussion

1. When you use the word miracle, do you often use it in a commonplace way, such as, "It's a miracle that I found a parking place"? What does that commonplace usage tell you?

2. What is your understanding of miracles? Do you know anyone who has experienced what you would consider a miracle?

3. What role do you think prayer has in healing?

4. When you've been ill, what suggestions about healing have been hurtful? What rituals of healing have been helpful to you?

5. What examples can you think of that reflect the difference between denial of death and "denial" on behalf of life?

6. Do you think people should everyone do their own funeral service before they die? Why or why not?

* * *

A PRAYER FOR TRUST

Let us learn that there is more than one kind of miracle, and that some miracles are as profound as the next breath we take. May we find the miracle that is less a cure than a resounding return of trust and faith. Amen.

What Is Our Part?

THE WOMAN WITH THE HEMORRHAGE

Now there was a woman who had been suffering from hemorrhages for twelve years. She had endured much under many physicians, and had spent all that she had; and she was no better, but rather grew worse. She had heard about Jesus, and came up behind him in the crowd and touched his cloak, for she said, "If I but touch his clothes, I will be made well." Immediately her hemorrhage stopped; and she felt in her body that she was healed of her disease.

Immediately aware that power had gone forth from him, Jesus turned about in the crowd and said, "Who touched my clothes?"...

The woman, knowing what happened to her, came in fear and trembling, fell down before him, and told him the whole truth.

[Jesus] said to her, "Daughter, your faith has made you well; go in peace, and be healed of your disease."

–Mark 5:25-31, 33-34

If Jesus had a signature "sign off," it was the phrase "Your faith has made you well." He said it to the woman who had been hemorrhaging for twelve years, to the blind beggar by the roadside, to the healed leper who returned to thank him. With this statement — your faith has made you well — Jesus veered away from miracles to the capacity to trust. He transferred power from the healer to the healed. The person who could replace a fearful hope for a cure with a trusting wellness became a healed person.

The impact and import of this statement is that *we participate in our own healing*. Put this into the context, for a moment, of the story of the woman with the twelve-year hemorrhage. She had apparently been trying for years to get better, going from one physician to the next, but instead of finding a cure, she only got worse.

This story has a particular resonance for many twenty-first-century readers. Many suffer — or know someone who suffers — chronic, debilitating illnesses. Some have not fully recovered from devastating accidents. Some have seen one physician after another, tried one treatment after another, and may have exhausted financial resources. Like the hemorrhaging woman, when all the medical advances do not work, when we reach the end of our rope, we are desperate to try anything.

This woman's story waves a red flag in front of our complaints and discouragements. Her shift to wellness began not with her "cure" but with her statement, *"If I but touch his clothes, I will be made well."* Notice the two parallel components: *faith* and *action*. She not only had to believe that her action would make a difference, she had to *take action*. She had to physically reach out her hand to touch Jesus.

In other words, we have to put our faith into action!

Don't get me wrong: I'm not saying that we should stop going to doctors and start trusting home remedies. But this woman's healing story clearly shows that we take part in our wellness. When we reach out, by our faith and our actions, we participate in our healing.

It may be something as simple as listening to the psalms if we cannot speak. Or listening to music if we cannot get to choir practice. Or saying one kind thing per day to those who care for us if we haven't the strength to speak.

Women with breast cancer might choose to participate in support groups. While studies show that this does not necessarily increase survival, these women have less pain, less anger, anxiety and depression.

The woman with the hemorrhage reached toward wholeness when she reached to touch Jesus' clothes. We're not talking about some wildly heroic action, or a costly action, or even a "sensible" action. We're talking about something as simple as touch. She put all her trust in the touch: *"If I but touch his clothes, I will be made well."*

Touch is a strong theme in the healing stories of Jesus:

And wherever he went, into villages or cities or farms, they laid the sick in the marketplaces, and begged him that they might touch even the fringe of his cloak; and all who touched it were healed.

–Mark 6:56

They came to Bethsaida. Some people brought a blind man to him and begged him to touch him. He took the blind man by the hand and led him out of the village; and when he had put saliva on his eyes and laid his hands on him, he asked him, "Can you see anything?" And the man looked up and said, "I can see people, but they look like trees, walking." Then Jesus laid his hands on his eyes again; and he looked intently and his sight was restored, and he saw everything clearly.

–Mark 8:22-25

People were bringing little children to him in order that he might touch them; and the disciples spoke sternly to them.

–Mark 10:13

And all in the crowd were trying to touch him, for power came out from him and healed all of them.

–Luke 6:19

We live in a world where touch is getting to be more and more of a "touchy" issue (sorry about the pun!). Teachers are instructed not to touch their students. Pastors are advised not to touch their parishioners and to keep their office doors open. I think we need to guard and protect the ancient rituals of touching.

When we lay on hands — whether it is as small as a gentle touch on the shoulder or as deep as an embrace of a sobbing person, holding hands and wires and tubes in a hospital bed, or a formal act — we imitate the way Jesus touched people.

The touch *is* the healing.

Putting faith into action initiates healing in many forms. The listening *is* the healing. The kind word *is* the healing. The support *is* the healing. Each of these is an action and an approach that shows that we have trust. Each of these is a plan for *wellness* — not a cure.

We all know that we will encounter sickness or dis-ease, that there is no special constituency for illness. Recognizing and readying for illness that will come our way can be an act of healing itself. Why should we not prepare to be sick — and also to be well — at the same time?

Our participation in wellness has not only spiritual and physical implications, but social as well — if you consider that one of biggest crises today is in the health care industry: lack of health insurance for millions, nursing shortages, debilitating liability suits against doctors...the list goes on. The most powerful solution is the wellness movement. It combines personal and social responsibility in an ethical way.

By wellness, I mean the intentional care of our person so that we avoid becoming a client of healthcare businesses in the first place. I mean exercising and eating thoughtfully, consuming foods that are more green, organic, and less environmentally and personally toxic. I mean drinking alcohol in a minimal way and avoiding smoking. I mean developing as stress-free a life as possible, using meditation, prayer, devotion, and simplicity as a life-style choice. Wearing a seat belt is also a form of wellness. These six choices — exercising, eating well, limiting alcohol, avoiding tobacco, reducing stress, and wearing seat belts — maximize health, both systemically and personally.

When I got sick with breast cancer, I learned something very important about myself: I hate going to the doctor. The offices have the least possible *feng shui*, to put it generously, and they always waste a chunk of my time. Even more, I hate being in hospitals. They are ugly, loud, and no place for a sick person. Once, after waiting for four hours for my insurance to approve a test my doctor had ordered, I began to scream at the receptionist: "The Health Care System is making me sick." There was truth in my loud, obnoxious-to-self-and-others lament.

While there are many solutions to the health care crisis that we could look at — reducing medical liability, increasing home health care, investigating the utopia of universal health care, treating health care as a right and as part of one's reward for labor — the best solution is wellness. We can start today and keep going on with it tomorrow. We can join the personal to the political. We can remove the "burden" on the institutions and shoulder a bit more of it ourselves. Wellness joins activism as an immediate and positive response to the crisis.

Wellness is what God hopes for us, not sickness. In that fundamental shift in the way we think about health care, we can solve its crisis.

Planning for wellness does not mean that we're planning *not* to get sick. Rather, it is a way of preparing ourselves for the day when sickness will come. It is a way of trusting in the power of Jesus to keep us spiritually well. We could surely develop our relationship with Jesus. We could study more scripture. We could pray more. We could imagine ourselves as those early Christians — who also had their own barriers to belief. Nothing like Jesus had ever happened to them before. At least we have the several centuries of a great cloud of witnesses!

By the way, remember "Tom," my friend in the previous chapter? As he crawled back to life from chemo, his first action was to request that our congregation replace the six pints of blood he had used. Replacing that blood helped us trust Jesus — and each other and Tom.

As we are able to trust Jesus' truth, we will find ourselves held by own capacity to hold on. (Or able to lean on each other to hold each other up!) Jesus is the one in whom we have the faith that makes us well. Jesus is the one we can trust even when others fail us. Jesus is the one we can trust after the best love of a family and community joins the best of medical care, the most positive attitude, prayer at its peak, and touch at its most tender — and still we find ourselves not cured, "only" well.

Questions for Reflection and Discussion

1. What do you think the role of faith is in healing?

2. How do you think touch relates to healing? What do you think of our culture's fears around the issue of touching?

3. When has touch made a difference in your well-being? Is there someone who could use your healing touch today?

4. What actions do you take to contribute to your wellness? What more could you do/would you like to do?

5. Are you more trusting or more suspicious as you get older? If you're more trusting, what has helped prepare you to trust? If you're more suspicious, what has brought you to this place?

6. Is there a hem on a garment for you somewhere? Is there something or someone you need to reach out and touch?

* * *

A Prayer for Trust

Remove us from the place called sick and tired into the place called well and motivated. Remove us from the place named suspicious into the place called trusting. Move us from the place where we can't be healed into a place where we can reach out and touch you. Amen.

SESSION FIVE

An Attitude of Gratitude

THE HEALING OF THE TEN LEPERS

On the way to Jerusalem Jesus was going through the region between Samaria and Galilee. As he entered a village, ten lepers approached him. Keeping their distance, they called out, saying, "Jesus, Master, have mercy on us!"

When he saw them, he said to them, "Go and show yourselves to the priests."

And as they went, they were made clean. Then one of them, when he saw that he was healed, turned back, praising God with a loud voice. He prostrated himself at Jesus' feet and thanked him. And he was a Samaritan.

Then Jesus asked, "Were not ten made clean? But the other nine, where are they? Was none of them found to return and give praise to God except this foreigner?"

Then he said to him, "Get up and go on your way; your faith has made you well."

–Luke 17:11-19

The story of the ten lepers raises an interesting question: Who was really *healed*? All of them had the same disease. All of them were cured. Yet only one person, the foreigner, returned to show gratitude to Jesus. The nine who didn't return might have had their leprosy cured, but the unique healing of Jesus could not touch them unless they returned to acknowledge him.

The nine who didn't express thanks were closed down before and after their disease, before and after their cure.

Although they were cured of their leprosy, they were still ill, spiritually, with ingratitude. They were closed to the light.

The one who returned was open to the light and therefore grateful.

Before you start mildly protesting that this story doesn't tell you much you don't already know — after all, your mother probably told you to write thank-you notes — consider this: When was the last time you wrote a thank-you note? Or meant to say "thank you" but then got busy and later felt embarrassed because so much time had passed, so you didn't say anything. Or who of us *hasn't* known a depth of gratitude for which we can never say thanks enough and then, somehow, end up not saying it at all? (I'm thinking spouses, children, siblings, best friends-the people we see all the time and find it too easy to take for granted.)

And what does all of this have to do with our healing?

Once I was in Hawaii for a week, and I made a game out of counting the many rainbows that came each day. One day I saw fourteen!

I said to my daughter late that afternoon, "Is it wrong to want to see one more today?"

She said, "Absolutely," and she was right. There is no point in greed.

Since cancer became the shark in my formerly serene swimming pool, I've made some shifts. For the cancer survivor, there is always the temptation to only look forward — to getting past the treatment, to counting the days, weeks, months, years of survival, to worrying about when it might show up again, to trying to make the most out of everything up ahead.

Looking forward, we can get greedy. Looking back, we can develop gratitude. There is a gratitude in looking back that is not possible in looking forward. This gratitude lets what days we have be full and good.

Otherwise the greed to see the fifteenth rainbow counts for more than the fourteen we've already enjoyed. We can get in our own way. By the grace of God, we can also get out of our own way. Indeed, we can move from greed to grace by braving our own excess. How? By learning to love what we have. By counting the rainbows we see every day. By making a life list of the multitudes of rainbows we've seen over the years. By focusing on being *full*, rather than getting *more*. By telling someone how grateful we are.

Gratitude for fullness often leads to a peace or tranquility. For this reason, one sailing at dusk on Biscayne Bay stands out in my memory. We had been out for about four hours when our captain turned toward home. Usually, in other sails, she had turned on the engine as we approached the dock because we needed to dock in a corner of the marina that was a bit of a tight squeeze, but not impossible with the engine running.

This night she got a twinkle in her eye as we turned toward home. "Let's try it without the engine. I think the conditions are right." But she wasn't quite sure, so she added, "We may have to turn the engine on at the last minute so be ready...we won't know till we get close."

Moments later we glided, soundlessly and effortlessly and enginelessly, into the berth. There was a calm in that moment that deserves respect and attention. It was quieter than I had heard, less effort than I had experienced, in a long time. Of all the sails on that bay, I remember this one — and I am thankful for it — the most because of the peace that attended it.

Effort is a persistent intruder in my life. Even getting to this sail had required large effort. I didn't know if I had the time, didn't know if it would be enough fun to warrant the time off, I wondered if I had brought the right dish for my part of the potluck, and so on.

Enginelessness, however, was an utterly new experience. Enginelessness is the other side of effortlessness; enginelessness is neither ease nor simplicity so much as the presence of peace.

This little experience caused me to revisit Jesus' words on abundance: *"I came that [you] may have life, and have it abundantly"* (John 10:10). I used to feel a bit mean toward them. "What's wrong," I would quip, "with just life? Isn't life good enough? Why the push for more and more?"

Nature writer and biologist Edward Hoagland believes that God created the world for the bubbles. For the froth. I like this idea. Perhaps abundance is frothy instead of functional.

The peace of enginelessness is also frothy. It moves us beyond the world of utility and "gotta gotta gotta." In other words, one sail like that particular night's sail is plenty. Having to work harder to get a bigger and better boat is too much. There is a difference between abundance and too much, and way too many of us know it.

Some people have figured out the way to engineless abundance. I think of the Italians who speak of the *sistemati,* or "settled way" of the evening stroll, the *passeggiatta.* They find purpose for life in the pursuit of beauty.

Turning off the engine is a good idea if we want peace or beauty or quiet in our life. Enginelessness is part of beauty. We know that Bach's concerti are beautiful as much because of what he left out as what he put in. But we don't have to "out Bach" Bach. We can be ordinary people living an ordinary life.

Sociologists join ordinary people in understanding how more is often less. I recently went to the store to buy a new pair of blue jeans. The clerk asked if I wanted slim fit, easy fit or relaxed fit, regular or faded, stone washed or acid washed, button fly or regular fly...and that's when I started to sputter. "Can't I just have a pair of blue jeans in my size?"

There are two kinds of people, according to Barry Schwartz in *The Paradox of Choice: Why More Is Less*: "Satisficers" and "Maximizers." Satisficers are those who are willing to live with the "good enough" rather than insisting on the best. Maximizers are people who are multi-tasking the world to its — and their — grave.

Maximizers are the half-empty cup people. They feel worse about loss than than any joy from gain, even if both loss and gain are equal. They forget nine compliments and only remember the one complaint. Some people just program themselves to always be brutally aware of what they are *not* getting. They have lost the ability to turn off the engine. They are closed to gratitude.

Turning off our engines gives us a capacity for quiet and opens us to the light of gratitude. It is a good way to live; engines are important some of the time but not all of the time.

Jesus *did* come so that we might have life and have it more profusely. Just as healing doesn't mean cure, abundance doesn't mean "more." It means that gratitude has crept into all the crevices of our lives.

We can achieve wellness in quiet ways, even at end times. We can be well when we're at peace. We can be well when we're on the road called gratitude.

Questions for Reflection and Discussion

1. Have you ever given something important to someone who never thanked you for it? How did you feel? What impact did this have on your relationship?

2. Think of a time when you received an extravagant gift and shared your outpouring of thanks with the giver. What impact did the sharing have on you? On your relationship with the giver?

3. Are there areas in your life where you feel "closed" to gratitude? What effect does this have on you? On your relationship(s)?

4. Where do you feel "greedy" for more? What are some things you could do to introduce an "engineless" quality to this area of your life?

5. What do you feel most grateful for these days?

6. To whom do you express this gratitude? Is there someone to whom you would like to "return to" to express your thanks?

* * *

A PRAYER OF GRATITUDE

How can we drink deeply from the well of gratitude? How can we be glad for what is? How can we enjoy what is here now rather than always insisting on the later sooner, the better, the more perfect? Give us a break from our perfectionism so that we can glean this Holy Present and your part in it. Let the last words on our lips at the end of every day — and at the end of our life — be, "Thanks be to God." Amen.